Alfred's **famous & fun** Piano Series **2**

early elementary to elementary

Christmas

12 Appealing Arrangements for Early Elementary to Elementary Pianists

Carol Matz

The playing of favorite Christmas music is a wonderful part of the holiday season. The arrangements in *Famous & Fun—Christmas, Book 2,* allow young piano students to contribute musically to the family's holiday traditions. This book can be used as a supplement to any method. No eighth notes or dotted-quarter rhythms are used, and there are only easy departures from five-finger patterns. The optional duet parts for teacher or parent add to the fun of playing the pieces. Enjoy your musical experience with these well-loved Christmas favorites!

Carol Matz

Alfred

Copyright © MMIV by Alfred Publishing Co., Inc.
All rights reserved.   Printed in USA.

It Came Upon the Midnight Clear

Words by Edmund H. Sears
Music by Richard S. Willis
Arr. by Carol Matz

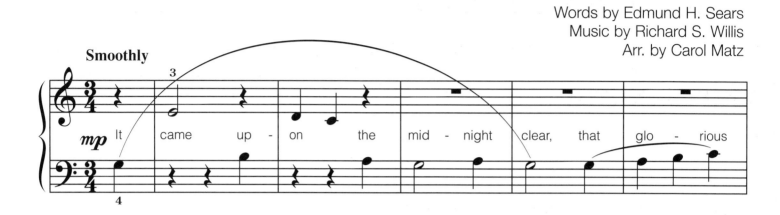

It came up-on the mid-night clear, that glo-rious

DUET PART (Student plays one octave higher)

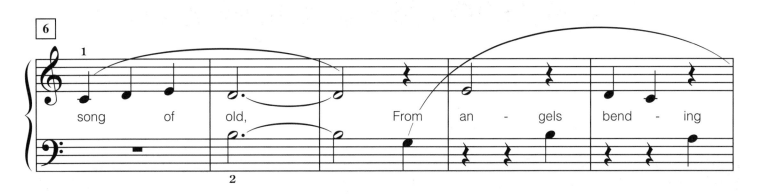

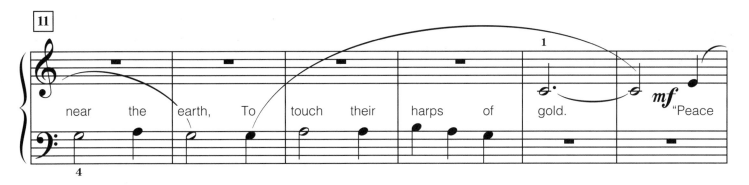

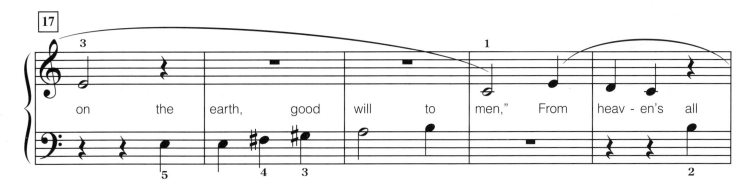

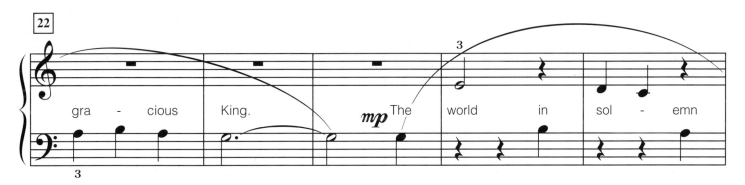

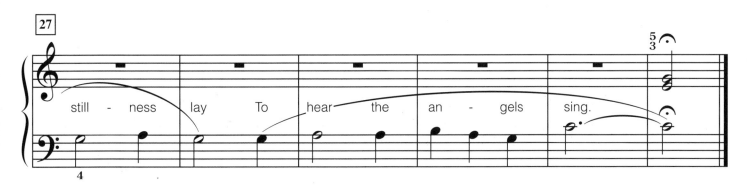

O Come, O Come, Emmanuel

13th-Century Plainsong
English lyrics by John M. Neale
Arr. by Carol Matz

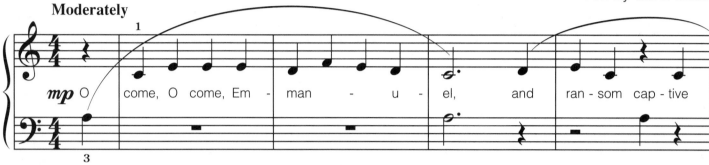

Moderately

O come, O come, Em - man - u - el, and ran - som cap - tive

DUET PART (Student plays one octave higher)

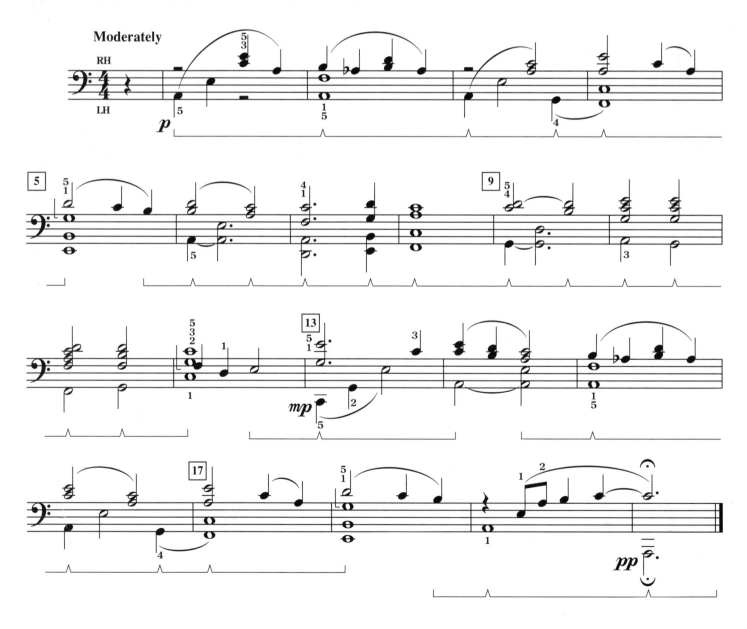

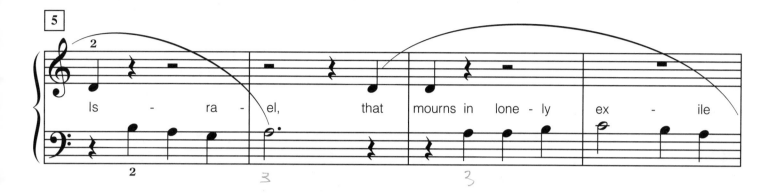

Is - ra - el, that mourns in lone - ly ex - ile

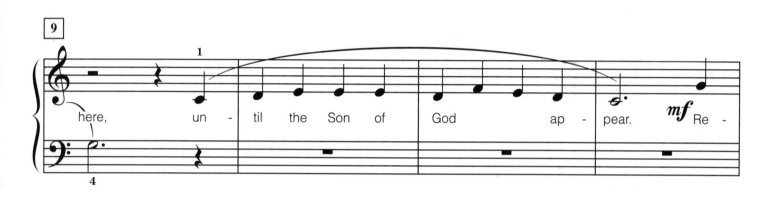

here, un - til the Son of God ap - pear. *mf* Re -

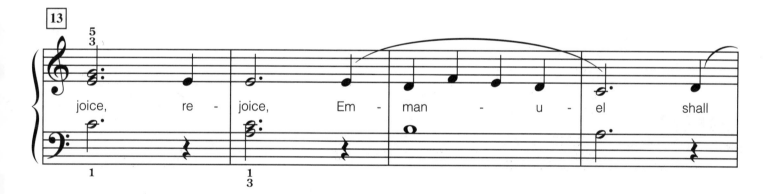

joice, re - joice, Em - man - u - el shall

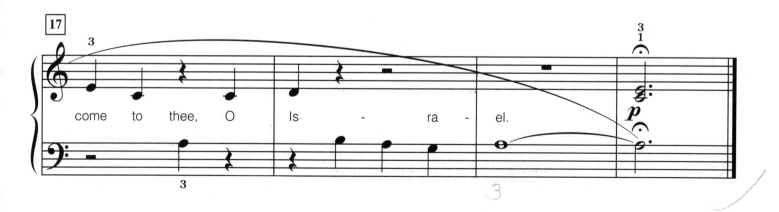

come to thee, O Is - ra - el.

Bring a Torch, Jeannette, Isabella

Traditional French Carol
Arr. by Carol Matz

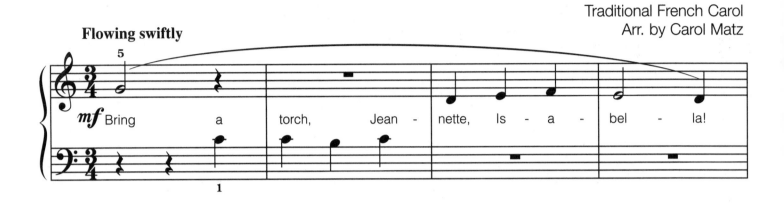

DUET PART (Student plays one octave higher)

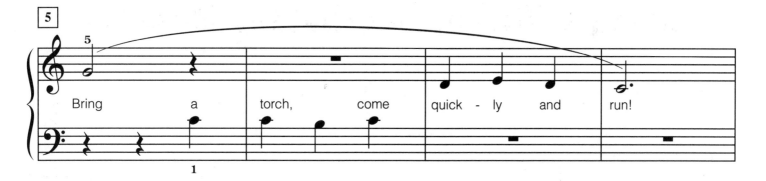

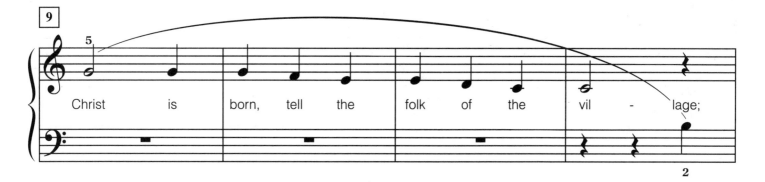

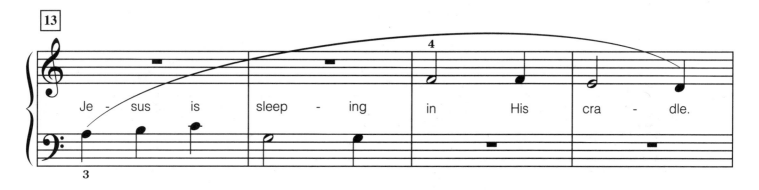

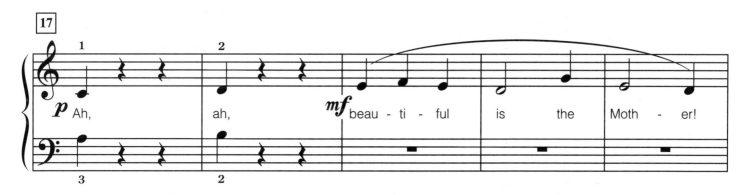

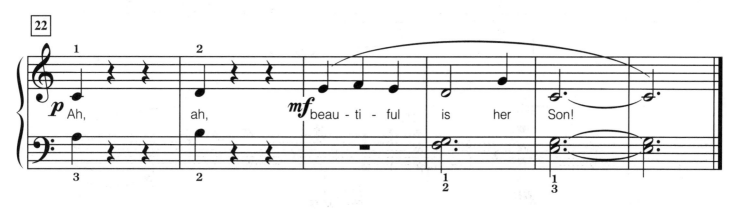

Joy to the World

Words by Isaac Watts
Music by George Frideric Handel
Arr. by Carol Matz

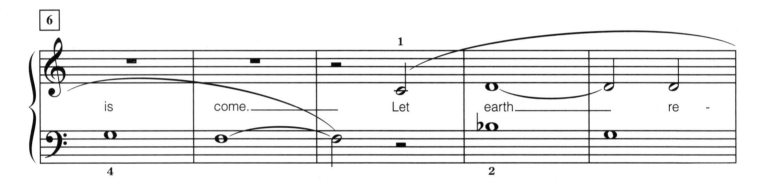

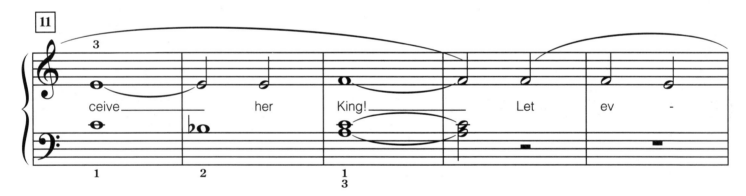

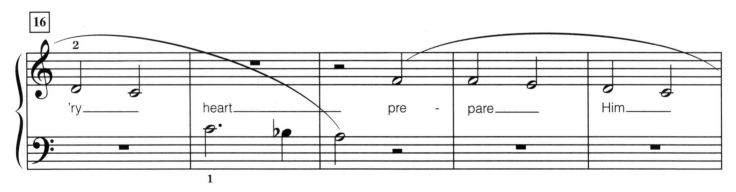

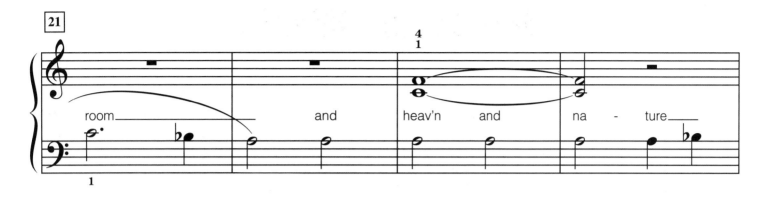

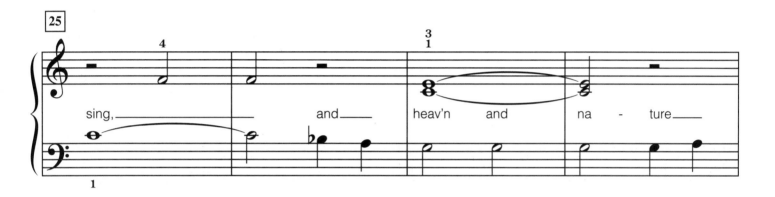

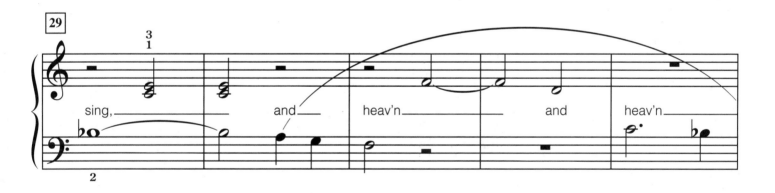

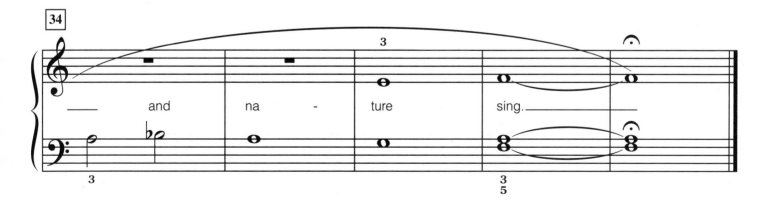

Ding, Dong, Merrily on High

Traditional French Carol
Arr. by Carol Matz

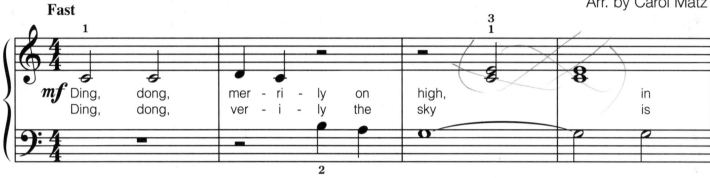

mf Ding, dong, mer - ri - ly on high, in
Ding, dong, ver - i - ly the sky is

DUET PART (Student plays one octave higher)

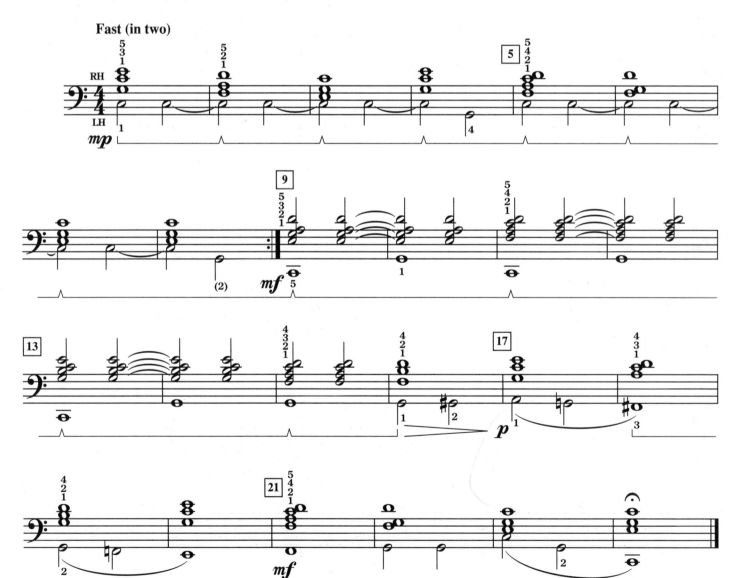

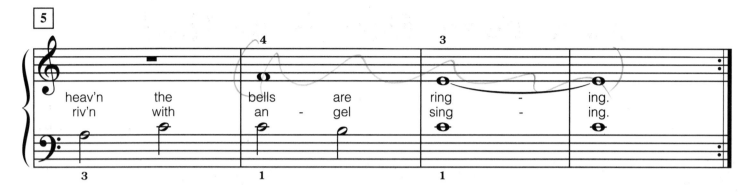

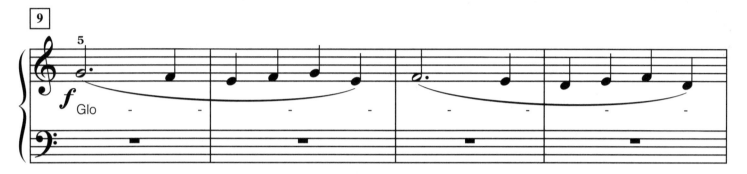

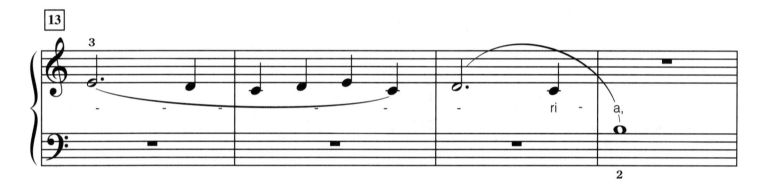

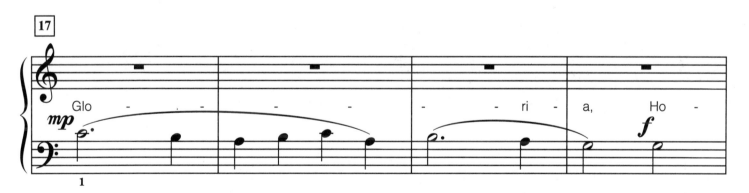

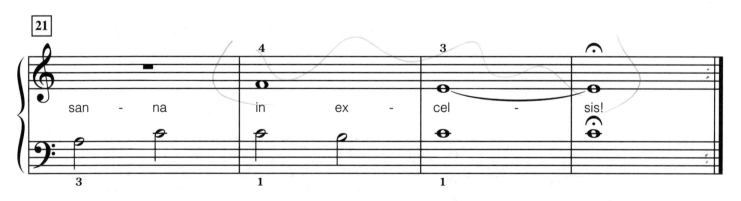

God Rest Ye Merry, Gentlemen

Traditional English Carol
Arr. by Carol Matz

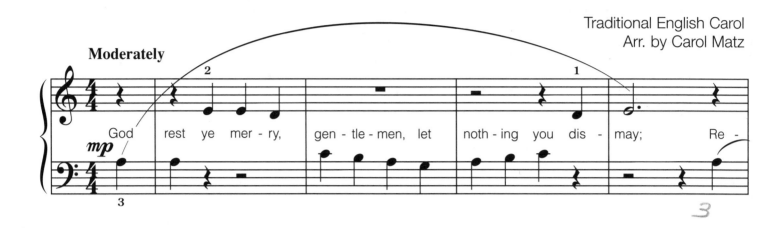

God rest ye mer - ry, gen - tle - men, let noth - ing you dis - may; Re -

DUET PART (Student plays one octave higher)

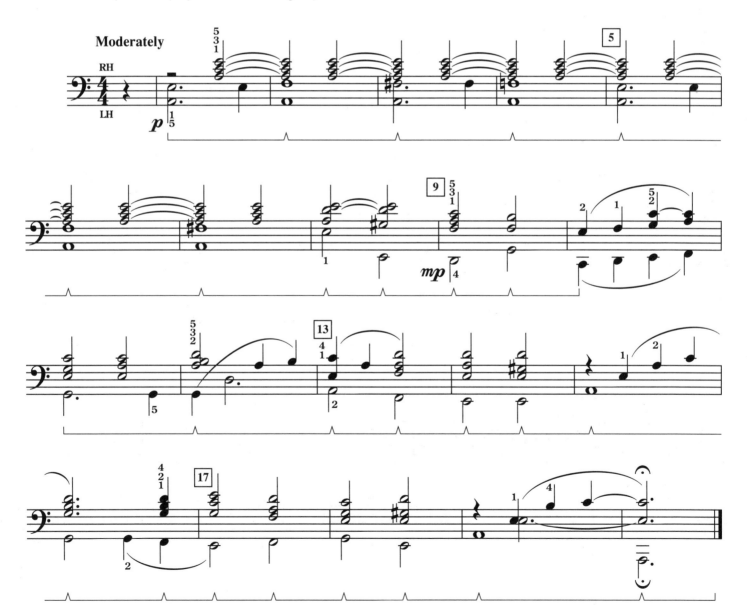

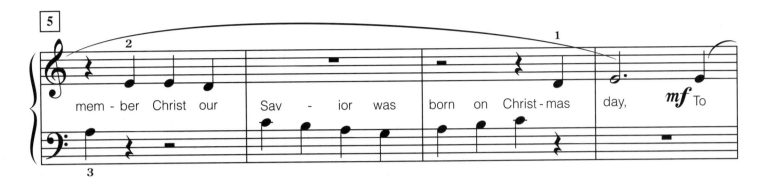

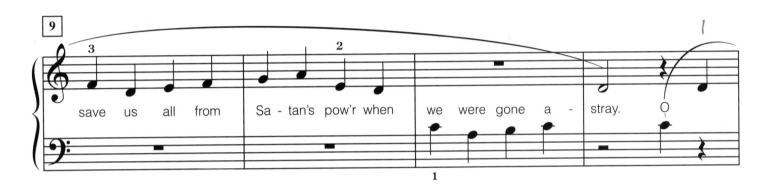

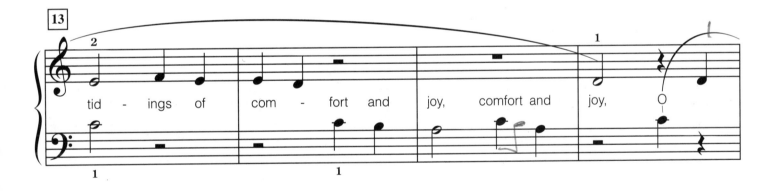

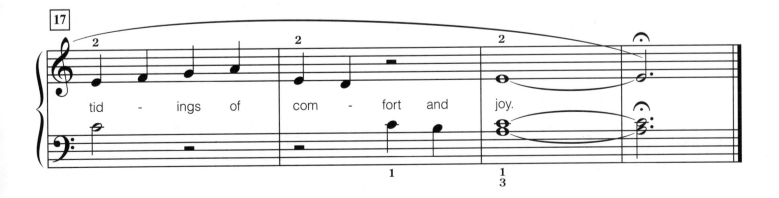

Here We Come a-Caroling

Traditional
Arr. by Carol Matz

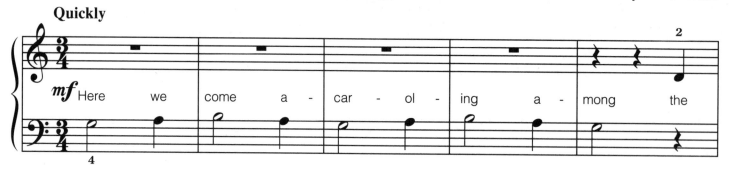

DUET PART (Student plays one octave higher)

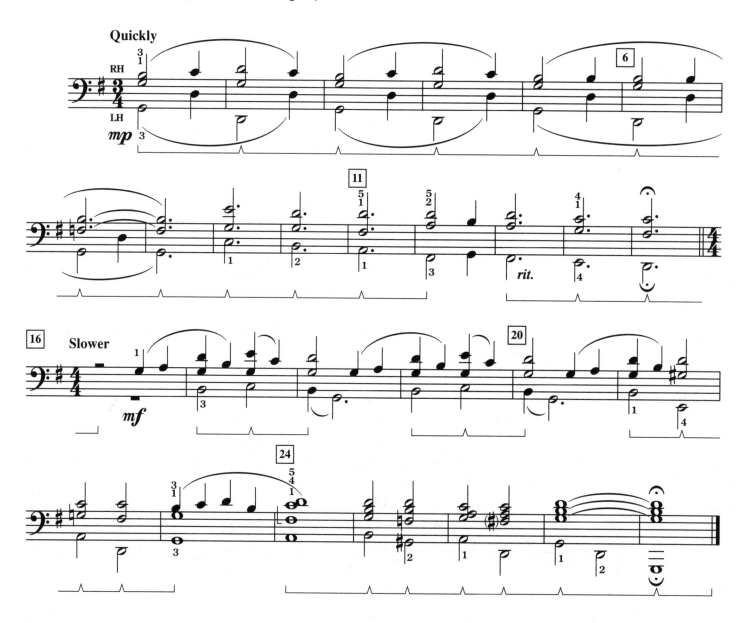

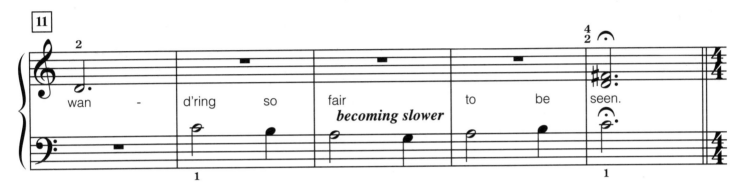

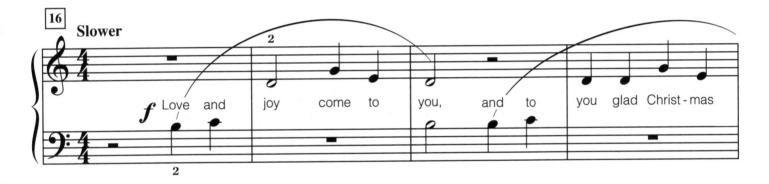

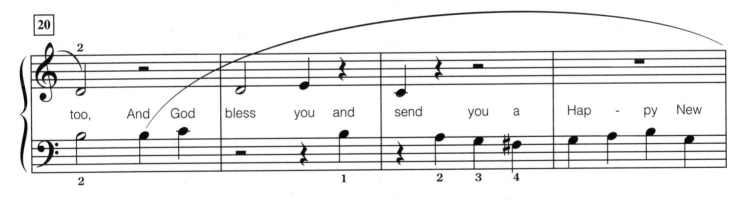

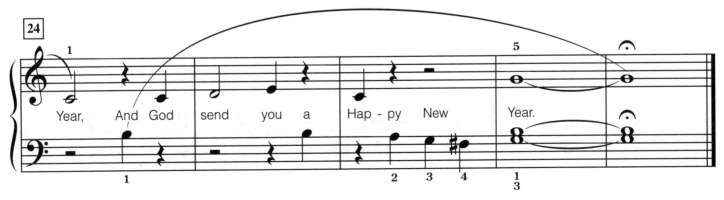

Jingle Bells

James Pierpont
Arr. by Carol Matz

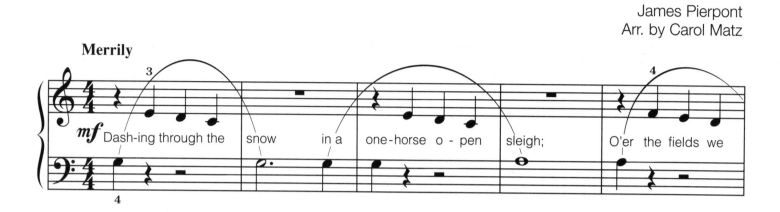

mf Dash-ing through the snow in a one-horse o - pen sleigh; O'er the fields we

DUET PART (Student plays one octave higher)

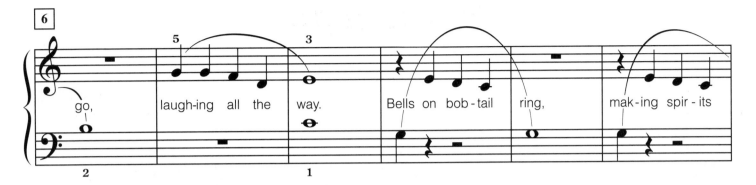

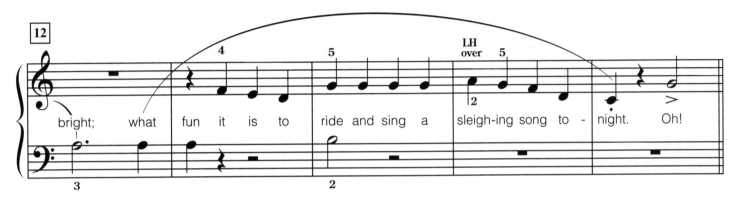

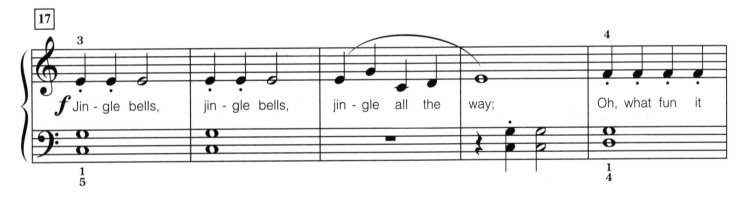

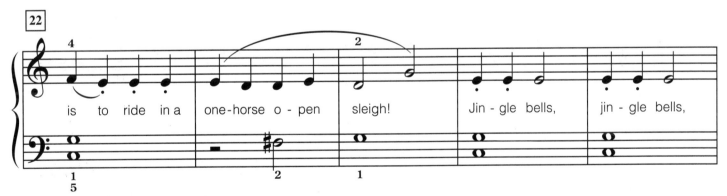

Dance of the Sugar-Plum Fairy

(from *The Nutcracker*)

Peter Ilyich Tchaikovsky
Arr. by Carol Matz

Quickly

Play both hands 2 octaves higher

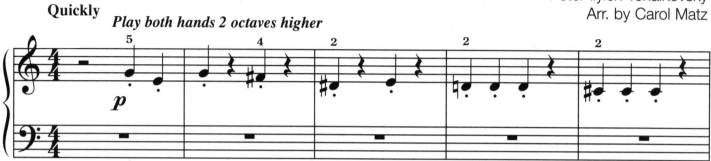

DUET PART (Student plays two octaves above Middle C)

Quickly (in two)

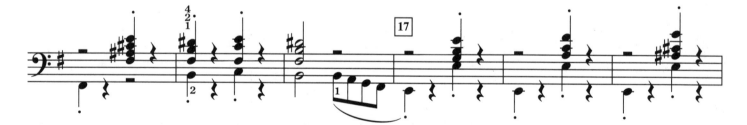

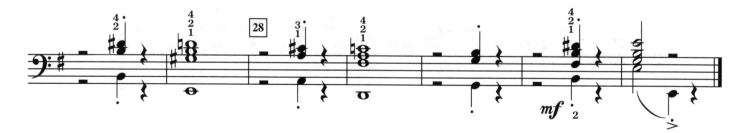

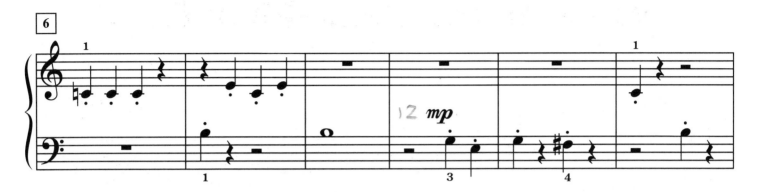

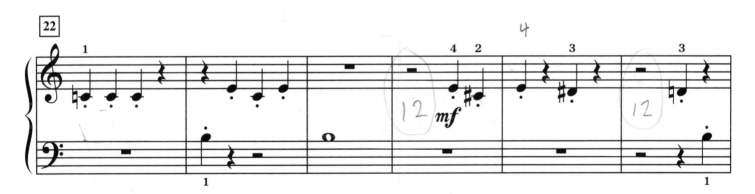

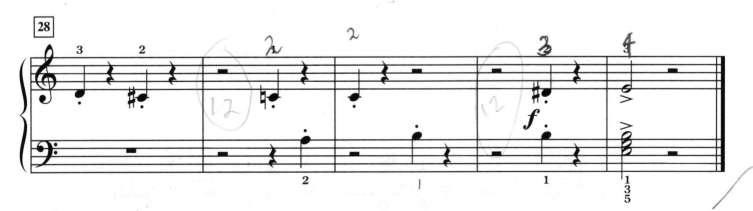

Angels We Have Heard on High

Traditional
Arr. by Carol Matz

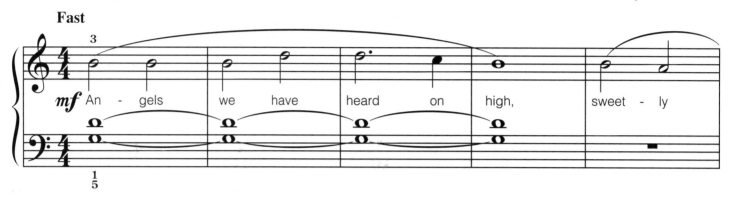

An - gels we have heard on high, sweet - ly

DUET PART (Student plays one octave higher)

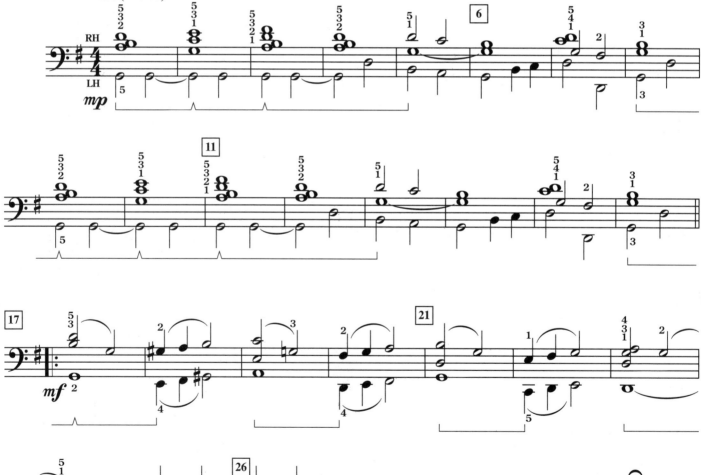

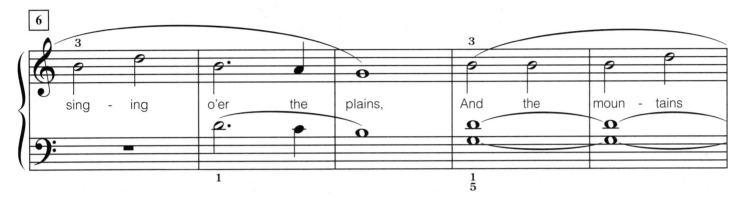

sing - ing o'er the plains, And the moun - tains

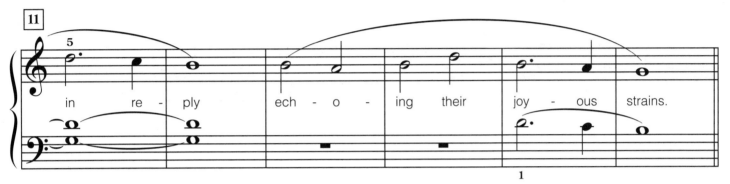

in re - ply ech - o - ing their joy - ous strains.

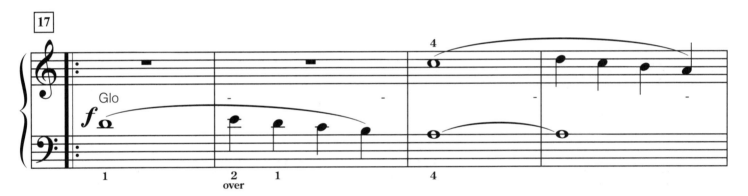

Glo - - - -

over

- - ri a { in ex -
{ in ex -

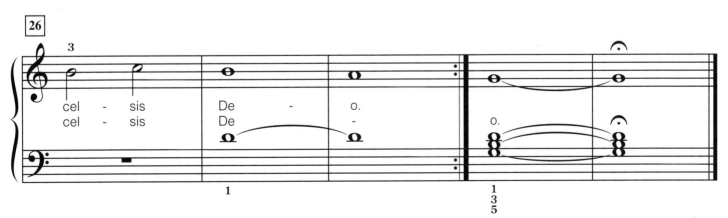

cel - sis De - o.
cel - sis De - - o.

Deck the Halls

Traditional
Arr. by Carol Matz

Festively, fast

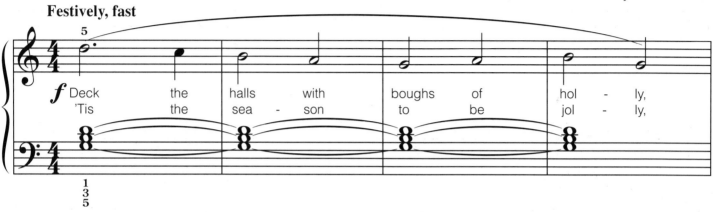

f Deck   the   halls   with   boughs   of   hol - ly,
'Tis   the   sea - son   to   be   jol - ly,

DUET PART (Student plays one octave higher)

Festively, fast (in two)

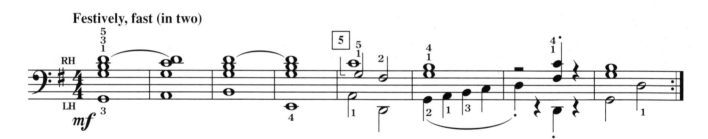

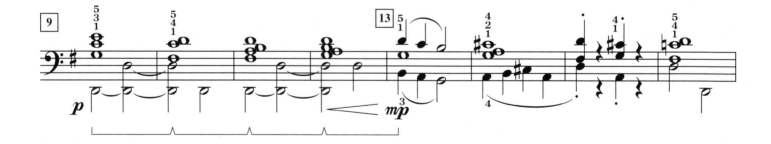

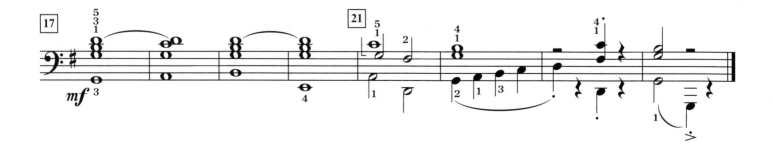

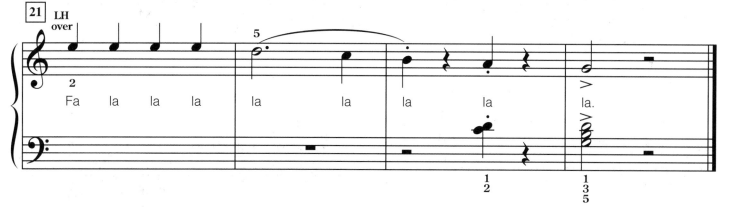

Coventry Carol

Traditional English Carol
Arr. by Carol Matz

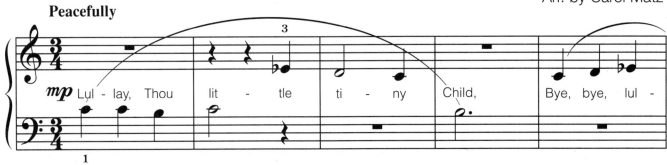

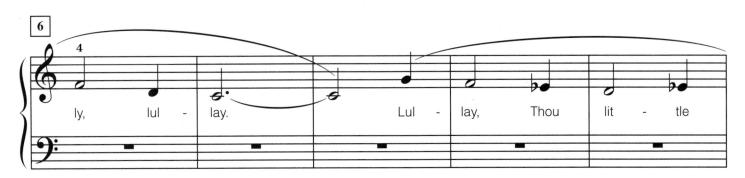

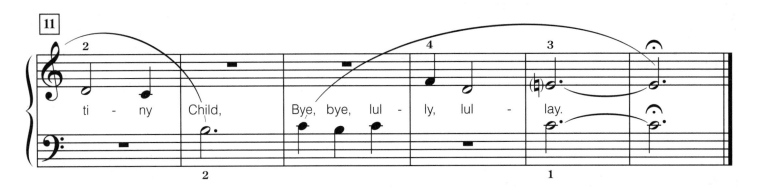

DUET PART (Student plays one octave higher)